KING VULTURE

KING VULTURE

POEMS BY
K. E. DUFFIN

THE UNIVERSITY OF
ARKANSAS PRESS
Fayetteville
2005

09 08 07 06 05   5 4 3 2 1

Designed by Liz Lester

∞ The paper used in this publication meets the mini-
mum requirements of the American National Standard
for Permanence of Paper for Printed Library Materials
Z39.48-1984.

LIBRARY OF CONGRESS
CATALOGING-IN-PUBLICATION DATA

Duffin, K. E.
    King vulture : poems / by K. E. Duffin.
      p.   cm.
    Includes bibliographical references.
    ISBN 1-55728-785-6 (alk. paper)
    I. Title.

    PS3604.U375K56 2005
    811'.54—dc22
                                2004022454

For Melissa Penny Chase

My only final friends—
the wren and thrush . . .
— HART CRANE

Acknowledgments

I gratefully acknowledge the following journals in which these poems first appeared, sometimes in a slightly different form.

"Wartime," *American Literary Review*; "Snapshot with Siberian Mammoth," *Atlanta Review*; "Lion," *Black Warrior Review*; "Birding in Yucatan" and "How the Crab *Iliad* Ends," *The Chariton Review*; "Those Decimated Hills," *Confrontation Magazine*; "Pangaea" and "Deer Hunt," *Cumberland Poetry Review*; "Brief History of a City," *Defined Providence*; "Opening Day," *Flyway*; "Reading Cyrillic," *Graham House Review*; "Harbor at Old Saybrook," "Generations," "Old Keys Highway," and "Endangered," *Harvard Review*; "Current Events," *Iron*; "Out Here," *Laurel Review*; "Goethe in Sicily," *Lines*; "Duplicity," *Literal Latte*; "Early Snow," *New Orleans Review;* "Posthumous," *North American Review*; "Goethe at Naples" and "Male," *Partisan Review*; "Bronze Age Helmet," *Poetry*; "*The Gallic Wars,*" *Prairie Schooner*; "Front," *Rattapallax*; "What They Said about Killer Bees," *Red Letter*; "Anatomy Class," "Climb," and "New England Summer," *The Sewanee Review*; "Canary," "Fireflies," and "Flood," *South Dakota Review;* "Seashore Movie, 1960," *Southeast Review*; "Deliveries," *Southwest Review*; "Fall," *Southern Humanities Review*; "Troy," *Sparrow*; "At Marconi Station," *Verse*; "Thunderstorm at the Zoo" and "What I Don't Know about Hippos," *Whiskey Island Magazine*.

I also wish to express my gratitude to The Millay Colony and Yaddo, where a number of the poems in this book were written.

"Goethe at Pompeii," "Goethe at Naples," "Goethe at the Colosseum," "Goethe in Sicily," and "Goethe at Girgenti" are based on the English translation by W.H. Auden and Elizabeth Mayer of *Italian Journey,* a collection of Goethe's letters published by North Point Press in 1982. A few phrases derived from this translation have been woven into my poems.

Contents

KING VULTURE

Bronze Age Helmet

The brow permanently furrowed in worry or alarm.
Impossible to bellow through the mouth's vertical dagger.
Eyes scrunched so close as if light would harm
the very concept of sight. Two boars who stagger

at your cheeks to sniff the scent of meat on your lips—
all of this metallic bluster undermined and denied
by those flower buds curling their incised tips
where rust begins around your vanished side

with its borders of herringbone so daintily stitched:
"But I'm-not-Herakles," is all you knew
when shimmering droves, like so many scissors to snip
the thread of your life, clamored like doubles toward you.

Columns shivered in the sun, and then were still,
turned to russet and verdigris on a hill.

TROY

And was it all true? Did black ships
the Greeks drew from Aulis and from Thisbe
of the Many Pigeons (who rise in fright today
making of the ruins a white-haired woman), slip
into that malevolent bay, where wind swirled
and hacked with its sword at the slanting walls of Troy?
Did she ever turn from the ramparts, sorry for a boy
whose glittering breastplate cracked like the fragile world
reflected in her eyes? How can we,
who saw thousands drown in a bloody sea,
who saw incandescent cities with ashen walls,
who took gruesome Hektor's photo at last,
not believe those bellowing Bronze Age skulls,
the sewn-shut eyes of Agamemnon's mask?

PERSEIDS

Evanescent plumblines flare and erase
themselves soundlessly behind the houses.
It's 2 a.m. on an August night and space
is suddenly bright as milk—the forest rouses,

churrying like a horde of manic clocks:
"KA—TY—DID. CRICK—ET."
What's left of the moon drifts and idly docks
in a graphite bay, slicking a gray picket

fence with sudden silver as lawns rustle
their colors into albums and decompose.
Like underworld butterflies, bats hustle
and batter the soft-nosed dark with their rapid blows.

Are the meteors stitching eulogies to sense
or making whole again a view that yields
to childhood tales of silent and immense
figures striding barren astral fields?

No melody hangs harp-like from his arms,
his vesper shrines are tame with austere blue.
But touching down, even now, on farms
that have always waited for a sign, are a few

embers from his sword. The sleeping earth
hasn't turned to stone. That face with gashes
on its stem is gone, for what it's worth.
Dawn hauls away the warm ashes.

MALE

Orion on his knees in the dusty-haired trees
    his mauve cloak of sky
    shrugging off its stars,

or beginning a frozen cartwheel after Taurus,
    that divining rod with eye
    of ruby rivaling Mars,

reminds us of the delicacy of men,
    who were never made for fire,
    mud, or vaults of sea

though history always packed them dumbly in,
    supple bodies for hire,
    a biomass for free,

leaving a few sketchy, starlit scars
    where the buried photos are
    of children along the shore

taught to name the bumbling hunter above,
    who leaps in his airless game
    after the map of a bull or stag,

a trapezoid whose corners slowly move
    through wastes of brutal fame,
    the sad shoulders tugged

on the rack of space in opposite directions,
    a blinking devolution
    without a human face.

HOW THE CRAB *ILIAD* ENDS

With beautifully patterned armor, like *Iliad* warriors,
Bronze Age crabs hunker near a windless battlement
and tensely survey a tidal pool whose hours
are numbered as relentless waves begin their ascent.

One gathers a blur of seaweed to its hammered breast,
then scuttles after another, the whole tribe
ferocious, each with horrid designs on the rest.
No wonder they're skittish when shadows only describe

a conspiring double whose jaws working above
the saffron chin—like a tough guy taking it in
before he lunges—mouth the absence of love.
Like tiny Trulli houses steeped in gin,

fractured barnacles await the slam of surf
where rust-colored patches across the bottom, more brilliant
than those on an old, junked De Soto, are the turf
contested on tip-toe with slow-motion feints

in a bloodless ballet sealed off from the prying sky.
Sun tinkers with the lighting and dapples the foes.
Suddenly a big hoplite sidles by,
his mouth stuffed with a limb, like a Thorazined Chronos.

The vanquished one, drab as an old tank,
descends a few tones and blends into the green

defeat of sunless water, missing a chunk,
the strange white flesh exposed—what does it mean?

No funeral fanfare. Starfish, like discarded corsages
of dusty rose, or splayed cartoon runners,
provide the missing exclamation that lodges
in a dark crevice of the soul. What honors

the dead in a wordless world where a burgundy sea
creeps up to submerge the place and all in the story?
What distinguishes *this* . . . from glory? The mood has soured.
In a cloud of sand, Hektor is dragged off and devoured—

WARTIME

A carnival tent no longer, my friend the sky
stomps off, wearing an ominous orange slicker
like a craggy fisherman told of a wreck nearby,
who threads among the rocks where waves flicker
and spit from a frothing sea. Mute and male,
deaf to chatter and reason, this is his chore:
brute and wordless motion, what he's for.
Women's noise is small to his arousal,
school is Lilliputian, art a crumb
he crushes obliviously beneath his boot
on his way to get the grim job done.
As lily-talkers sway in tidal pools,
he smirks that he's the one who knows the route
when only muscle and cunning fit the rules.

HUMMINGBIRD

Tiny upstart helicopter, ecstatic rotor,
whose intent is rowing a dragon's scaly jewels
with almost breaststroke—a faceted glinting shudders
the landscape of your throat from violet, to rose, to emerald,

then snuffs it to black the sun can't toy with or color.
You abruptly accelerate and fathom the cloudless—zoom,
a sleepless desire, stunning with the giddy soar
of a tinkerer, a tin whirlygig battering the whiteness of noon.

With zee-eee-eert you gobble up even tinier
air punctuation, a detour. Scimitar- or scythe-billed
against the light, turning from the shoulders to stare
with motor sound, gorget all scintillant and thrill,

you inspect the flower troops, a capped lieutenant.
Filibuster long. Then hang and swing slightly
from an invisible chinning bar—swing! Revenant,
loose-jointed swiveller, burning a darkness self-sized

in milk. A talent—not tentative—for hoisting suddenly
to stratospheric pine on invisible wire—like a deus
ex machina zipping back to Olympus by pulley.
Snipped free to decide—you veer a nanosecond and are lost.

Nothing frivolous, no excess in how you rent the sky.
Not a babbler or a dabbler. A doer with a pinpoint eye.

CANARY

Trills like something being asked for verging on sobs
that swerve into belted-out arias, far too big
for a bird. From your hanging cage, you can't hob-nob
with the gabbling and chiming sparrows; besides, your wig

of orange would scare the daylights out of them.
Are you Figaro One, or Figaro Two? I knew
to name you so. The ones who came after (ahem)
were Pumpkin the First and Pumpkin the Second, who flew

out of this world in various ways: stung
by a bee, or knocked from a perch by a heart attack
so small no one could see how the delicate veins

had shuddered to still-life, as in a Dutch painting,
where a dead goldfinch, its gaudy body gone slack,
hangs over the edge and its blood, like music, drains.

Snapshot with Siberian Mammoth

Pincer action, a gem of a strategy
for so many generals, illustrated here in ivory.
Darth Vader's helmet. New Guinea nose.
Bone as pugilist. The dog-like toes.
Whatever match struck and flared in his puffball
of a cranium, where eyes of rainbow jasper smoldered,
has guttered and gone out—whatever's old, he's older.
Finger the abacus of spine and tail,
those barrel staves of rib to hold the rum
of a life which long ago dribbled out onto snow.
An Ice Age funeral parlor or museum?
A lugubrious curtain makes it hard to know.
Posing beyond his reach, we have that grin
of having escaped—for now—the gathering in.

DEER HUNT

Each print, a deep, cobalt pointing
ahead like a doubled needle on a white compass.
See how they sink so firmly, sure of the grass
beneath the snow if nothing else, anointing

the air with fear, their beautiful coats out of Dürer,
and muzzles dipped in glossy India ink.
In their eyes, a vestige of a thought they cannot think.
Quivering, they feel it closing in from those purer

slopes they fled. Here they mill and bed
by night in scattered thickets, turning and murmuring
near the frozen stream. They've heard the hills condemn

their steaming breath and in the frail light, dread
like a pointed stick prods them on—that thundering
in the distance with which the forest turned on them.

OTHER

Remember *Zinjanthropus* of Olduvai,
inscribed in a tear-stained book of distant storms.
Cathedral of jaw and famished, sunken eye,
one of the burly, disinherited forms,
a name no longer furled in quivering marrow,
but muttered by paleontologists asleep
in Latinate rooms as they dream of life's harrow
churning up a skull buried deep,
whose profile veered toward human and away,
then slowed among the ones we had to banish
because he never shaped a stone with stone.
His stunned gaze, beneath a brow of gray,
follows us across the Gorge to where we vanish,
along with the terrible syntax for "alone."

ANATOMY CLASS

For Andrew Syrbick

You begin to be familiar with the dead,
how their minds grow small and leathery,
how the invisible bellows of the rib cage, bled
of breath, becomes a slatted ovoid sea,
a louvered egg, as form mumbles its lines,
a shambles of shadow and bared articulation.
This flensing and flaying to sway-backed spine
and vanished eye in its frangible chalky cavern
is how the world falls away from the knife
of time, leaving scattered drawings pinned
where a furtive pulse sped to fluttering white:
a barium moon swallowed by tolerable night,
a viny, strangling hand of winter wind,
a talc of sun dusting foreshortened life.

GROVE

Where snuffed-out candles of pine beckon to blue,
their sleeves billowing and rustling in a fragrant wind,
there you will find the sunken pool, its hue
black as tar, and the swallowed stars within.
Small gatherings of debris make fragile camp,
and these years no one comes without flashlight or lamp,
only the wind and the plump cerulean jays,
their crests like fabulous sails from *Odyssey* days.
The air, like a small dog that grew to a greyhound's
starved form, pads through with hardly a sound.

Top-knotted like a tiny samurai,
Cupid frowns toward the road, wearing the profile
of a nineteenth-century girl—the brow so high,
of pockmarked stone, the occult inward smile.
Not whitely sculpted of salt, as at a child's grave,
but more like the shaped earth looking at itself
and the field beyond—an impossible erotic glance
over the shoulder of time, where nothing can be saved.
Far off, a Roman light scatters its wealth,
and what falls where, falls by the laws of chance.

A headless nymph, like an Olmec god, hides,
crouching by the pool, disturbed by the shushing of the pines—
for it sounds like cars coming slowly up the drive,
and people who have vanished, with all their festive signs
of arrival on a summer day. But November's sway
is eternal. The quilt of needles drawn up will stay

and thicken, and the concrete benches spangled with pebbles
will continue to flake away like chert or fossils.
See how they tilt already as the ground softens
to engulf what was once well-made and gulp it in.

And a bird bath, like a martini glass of stone
tilts too, as if to offer darkened water
to a thirsty sky, as an anaconda vine
sinuously clings to a leaning shack where a bar
is now a driftwood wreck with rusted chicken wire.
All the colors—and surely there were colors—have gone,
like garish pigments from ancient statues, worn
by the rains and suns and snows of fifty years.
All blending now to the democratic tones
of forest everywhere, and anonymous bones.

What to make of a door hinged to a tree,
whose fence or gate is gone—utterly?
Green with the million silvery greens of spring,
it cannot open now, but keeps subsiding
into the forest floor, defining a house
of air. Think of the stoicism of houses,
whose black-bordered eyes are always prepared for loss
and never show surprise: here is their ghost,
whose windows flared at noon and flushed at dusk,
surviving all inhabitants without remorse.

O rare vintage as good as poured into sea.
The living pelt of the world dissolves in stages.
The pool has lost its human clock and ages

like a rock formation, imperceptibly.
We praise what is classical but not the cost,
how it comes about: the sluggish tide of earth
washing the corpse and the fabulous, lulling moss
in brilliant mats that overtakes the birth
of whatever we build. And syllables come of this,
the remnant, in the end, of whatever this life is.

LION

Like granite at evening, with heart of arctic chill
you lie, still and sculpted in the mind,
facing elsewhere, a minor oracle
of birds gathering at your paws to find,
in their massive puzzle, the last confectioner's crumb.
As the coroner of clouds is herding west
those salubrious fibs of color, past the slum
of beryl-dipped buildings, toward their rest,
a convalescent shadow creeps across
what you've become: eyes of bleached stone
fixed on silver pools of absolution,
parks of papery leaves that flutter loss.
And I am no one, watching night begin
to fleck your coiled flanks with dissolution.

THE CARTOGRAPHER

For Richard Edes Harrison

He and I were sign painters in the kindling sun,
coaxing the luster of black ink onto white
board to label quadrants on a minuscule island.
He showed what could be elegant and right,

after the world was no longer elegant and right.
Nips from a hip flask, his only concession
as he mapped the unknown small against the night,
and barked his brilliant notes of ditty and reason.

He squeezed Mercator, giving earth its volume,
all the while maroon coffin-shaped crosses
the color of dried blood in his mind were losses
to the same earth that bucked and smothered: a tomb.

Longitude and latitude he graphed
and played like strings, a master of deletion,
his spare drawings with rapidograph, like math,
made places where all was forgiven and unbegun.

My sole apprenticeship in that first season
when to say "I am" and have the world agree
seemed the greatest mystery. Like a son
I trailed the master's neat calligraphy—

heard 45s breathe Bach like a feather across keys,
and saw through old binocs the jaeger swoop
among the shattered jade of choppy seas—
as he made a serif, then a glistening loop.

Thirty years ago, and I've not become
the mapper he'd admire: where grasses awaken
we're painting still though he's gone, his life a sum.
In the end, a niche is taken or forsaken.

Old Foundation

It will look like this when it happens. Without a cry.
A crypt or cradle the length of a minor church
filled with the haywire prayer of aspiring trees,
a slow conflagration lit by the sun's torch,

breaking down the colors to browns and grays,
intent on forgetting whatever it used to hold
and going under as vines lash the cold
edges where sowbugs breed and scuttle away.

A doorframe hangs askew between two cartoon
windows, and even the air stoops to get through.
A drainpipe's silent mouthing of a vowel
warns that soon it won't be possible

to tell the outside from the in
and whether something has vanished or arisen.

THOSE DECIMATED HILLS

Decay is a tone that children hear, a humming
of rancid smells and sour milk, the taste
of mold—the depredations, the braiding in
and reaching through of what is being lost.

Calling, calling. Several small birds
who would not survive the winter, tossing leaves
beneath our rhododendron which still grieves
for their shadows, though it, too, has disappeared.

And the great tree—soon to be hacked out,
leaving a crop circle of blue gravel
naked in the light pouring its rivulets
like acid—fluttering the last red spell

of its life. Children see how adults look away
from those decimated hills that are the other
side of birth, dreaming of a sister or brother
lost. Children know what they do not say.

Pets turning to mulch in flesh-colored woods.
The stillness. The ticking. Time like a stained ribbon
folded on the breast of day stiff in its coffin.
Such things are very close and understood,

like the ruffed grouse beneath the window, mute,
its neck freakishly supple, with a dark ring,
one red bubble no longer pulsing
in the small nostril, hole in a bloodied flute.

POSTHUMOUS

Just as the sinking sun became invisible,
cumulus clouds were punched up very white
as if forgetful day decided to ignite
and the lesson once again was legible:

to everything is granted an afterglow,
but the trick is to see it before its threatened hour
is displayed, translucent, in a funerary jar,
like the wasp on the sill, a winged embryo

with burnt antennae and bridal veils of smoked honey,
furled transparent maps whose veined patterns
no one knew, the raspy legs drawn high
as if to protect the helmeted face of satin

from what was once the brink—yesterday,
when I hardly noticed it trapped in the window bay.

Threescore and Six

For Richard Curry Marius

Fluorescent lifejackets appeared on the crest of a hill,
bobbing like buoys in the heated air: a whole
sailing family, stranded in a violent squall,
glimmering toward me like giants with shadows of coal.

You were not among them, though I tried to save you there,
in that lucky platoon remembered from decades past,
but your watch was already loose around your wrist,
your orator's voice diminished to a muffled quaver.

*"Vanity of vanities, saith the Preacher, vanity
of vanities; all is vanity."* The body's season
is gone, your form dissolved in a reachless sea,
rhetoric ribboning away on its own mission.

I glimpsed you last as father of yourself.
When the cold cozening of illness furled you in,
silencing your stories, seizing your verbal wealth,
I felt—how strange to have felt this—like an orphan.

Neutral light reads from your open book.
Dead as Scott in his tent. The astonishment.
Not to be found beyond words, wherever we look.
The only letter between us, this one. Unsent.

Preparing for the Afterlife

It's already begun: in leathery veins da Vinci
sketched with ink like dried blood, the journey
no one wants to make from infancy,

where the living shudder and dissolve into shrunken brown
bones or bits of tissue that never drown
in jars of formaldehyde like pharaohs brought down

and hacked in dank basements, things we admired
as if they had nothing to do with us, happily tired
from voracious museum visits to see shrouds fired

in the kiln of earth with their embarrassing henna stains
like rust patterns on an old ceiling where the rains
seep, whatever the canopic jar contains,

the body, contracted like a beggar's foot in rags,
severed forever from impulse as it drags
across the sand, cloth fluttering like flags,

but only in the mind, in tales we were never fed—
the clump, clump of the sick man not picking up his bed,
but dying and walking into the desert instead.

KING VULTURE

On currents, on thermals—*Sarcoramphus papa*—
you float above a faded strip of forest,
small pilot-head in baroque regalia,
helmet of layered colors, snug leather mask

with eye-holes cut out over tangerine red,
avocado pit pendant from your breast spun
of silk, dipped-in-ink fingers spread
above the startled trees like a benediction.

You drift in and out of worlds as we do,
always looking for the dead, who outnumber us
beyond imagination. An eternal video.
We are their orphans, made of video and dust.

Eyes of white sky soaring over ruins,
I have collected you. How fabulous you were
in your priestly robes, picking the world clean.
My young world. Bone scanner and surveyor.

Your cousins huddle and hop in airy cages.
Like the banner of a vanquished army, you still drift,
scanning cloud mausoleums through the ages,
each washed-out cerulean day a gift.

Pictor. Seer. Knowing air, flesh, and vision.
Your silence, retinal splendor, majestic nod.
Preserving all by dismantling all precision—
your desire strangely close to the mind of God.

GOETHE AT POMPEII

Models for architects, or dollhouses,
windowless, the sun loitering at their cave maws,
buildings here are toys. The city surprises
a northern temperament: our coolness thaws,
for the remnant heat within can still be sensed.
Before long, we're flustered and miniaturized.
Peeling frescoes ringed by arabesques
adorn arcades barely human-sized
where nymphs and children prance to silent pipes.
Animals, wild and tame, weave in and out
of wreaths on fractured walls as the air wipes
blistered paint from fading forests. I doubt
that we can ever comprehend such love
of art, given the cautious way we live.

The ghostly sectors left me feeling grim
so I sought an old escape route to the sea
crinkling beneath the sky's azure rim,
and from the coast, surveyed this parched country.
(Later in Naples I saw tiny homes
like those at Pompeii, dark and neat, furnished
with floral chests, above-ground catacombs.)
It seems that stone and ash were suddenly unleashed
and clogged the city meters above its plinths.
Beneath the Vesuvial shadow in which art
had grown so extravagantly, through labyrinths
of centuries, disaster played the part
of time all too well. It's ironic, I know,
but think of a mountain village smothered in snow.

BIRDING IN YUCATAN

I remember a yellow-tailed oriole, stiffened on the road
outside Pueblo Nuevo, like a sick heart
stilled, a fallen butterfly dropped cold,
mid-beat, a phosphorescent spurt

of the venous blood of evening seeping in
where squat temples and tangled trees murmured
their crimes, intoning crude lists of slaughter
whose thrilling antiquity somehow absolved them of sin.

I made a watercolor sketch of the corpse—its black
bib and sealed eyes, which I opened, its tanager
blaze of blue on the bill—announcing *tropic*.
I'm startled now by how crudely it was rendered.

I was eighteen when I saw the bedraggled ponies,
brachycephalic Mayans in their white robes,
blue-black grassquits on the highway to Progreso,
leaping—*Volatinia*—from a field like fleas.

Time, not yet a luxury or a disease,
was simply a way of getting to a better place,
an impatience to be shed or endured. Often a race.
My companions called out the names of birds urgently,

each trying to be the first, and I lost,
unprepared for the game, unaware of the rules:

how hard they had studied for this moment and what it had cost.
This was the first of many dismantled schools.

In a black book whose pages were crinkled like waves,
I copied down, like dictation, their daily lists.
I was least of the group—given how scientists behave
my place became the shadows where I wasn't missed.

As motorcycles gunned below my window, I wrote
"A multi-colored line of Mexican draftees
straggled through the hot streets today and I thought
of all the slaves who built Uxmal." A breeze

rattled the shade, and a roach the size of a mouse
rattled the glass upended over the drain.
"Time is a much more arbitrary dimension
than distance," I wrote in script so tiny and precise

I no longer recognize it as my own.
I sent long letters full of enthusiasms and sketches
to people who never answered. In that old room,
the louvered clock I would leave behind inches

the hours. My parents are barely fifty, and the dead
are alive, feasting in droves. New species of birds
one of our group would discover, are unrecorded
on Andean peaks, and a single unfinished word

ends whatever I have to say in my book,
whose pages—after the first thirteen—remain blank

for twenty-eight years. The oriole's eye seems to blink,
accusing me of something, a failure to look

at the world more deeply, and apart. To accept that what I thought
I could become and what would really happen had begun
to diverge, the way the bird's life had been caught
and strangely preserved in paint though the bird was gone.

On April 5, 1973
I was eighteen and the yellow-tailed oriole, cold
and brilliant on the road, unknowingly entered history's
arbitrary dimension, where it never grew old.

THE GALLIC WARS

Participles gleam, like dull swords sunk
in clabbered mud. The clock flinches toward noon.
Caesar in his spattered skirt wars with swank
Caesar, cleanly reminiscing in his seaside home,

like a professor I would meet next fall at school.
Chains on tires like gladiatorial gear
ching in the slush of winter. We're the Gauls.
Or are we the Romans? Hueys drone and batter

Asian jungles where boys a year or two older
are sent if their numbers are low. But no one speaks
of fate or power or helplessness, the ominous folder
of plans others will have for us whether we're weak

or strong. We spent that year on strategy
as the legions closed in, crunching the lawns,
hunkering down in the doomed forests where we played,
their capes hidden by cold tree trunks at dawn.

Wordlessly our parents drove the roads,
full of nonsensical pride at our *beginning,*
never guessing how it would end, with epodes
about never having begun, about time hunting

us down, the fires of our doomed camps in snow
smoldering as our haggard retreating bands cross
what's left of suburban fields. Stunned, we show
them our withered forms: "O how could there be *such a loss?*"

THUNDERSTORM AT THE ZOO

Trees are waving from their hilltop raft for rescue,
twigs shaking like so many admonitions
from palsied scribes as the last torn blue
of the sky is hustled away by gray battalions.

The sheep have human voices, their maas and ahs
flat and full of the copperlight of harm,
stamping and jostling their roped-in beds of straw,
as when the *golem* enters the midnight barn.

A shortcut leads to where the lions prowl,
St. Jerome's cell blown open, man and beast
vanished. The rippling grass begins to growl
as raindrops spatter and quicken from the east.

Behind the veil of monsoon, a zebra stands
unalarmed in a field, his stripes jagged bolts.
A sodden ostrich flattens itself to the ground,
snaking its tiny head to peer at volts

that ransack nearby towns and snuff the lights.
Fire engines whoop and wail from all directions,
as rain batters like BBs and summer sleet.
In the ozoned forest, a flurry of electrocutions.

Earth is exposed as a tinderbox of fears.
The rheostat is suddenly turned way up.
With a huge crack, the zebra disappears,
leaving only a distant tattoo of gallop.

What I Don't Know about Hippos

With an umber eye like a grandmother's, but twice the size,
hoisted like a rubbery periscope, waterproof and slick,
is he kindly, oblivious, or plotting someone's demise?
Huge-headed, he flounders from the pool and it's a shock

to see him waddle down the road on his inscrutable mission,
a cameo in a nightmare where his smile suddenly comes loose
and hovers, Cheshire-like, before the stun
of a charge in full African sun by this . . . caboose.

"The horror!" We can't decipher his face or intent
so invent a plot as light butters all his folds.
Now he's back. Bucks and splashes. Content
to flaunt huge tusks, a murky lithograph rolled

in mud, he turns away to mangle a leaf
on shore, safely sealed off from us by glass.
On land he's ponderously, painfully slow on his feet,
but under water, he does a barrel roll fast,

his Flintstone mug beneath the meniscus, stubbly.
From *Fantasia*, or *Apocalypse Now*, a fatted cow
of molded plasticine, glistening. "Admire my jelly,
see me," is what he's thinking. I don't know how.

A nearby hand-lettered sign says "More people
are killed by hippos than by Cape buffalo or lions."

It seems a sin or just ridiculously simple
to attribute rage or delight to this feral scion

of pure bulk—though projection is unavoidable
when that human gaze trapped beneath swiveling ears
suddenly surfaces and stares—and the head rears,
the mouth yawning to bellow a monstrous syllable.

OUT HERE

Imagine the Sound with peaks of waves, frozen.
Somewhere, a metallic tapping miles away.
Smoke drifting up. Then you see a dozen
or so tiny figures pulling a sleigh

over what the water has become, trusting
the white thickness to hold and bear their weight
too, though no one else has been out here since a gusting
storm shaped and held each wave to its height.

Scattered iceboats are marooned like bits of crayon.
Think of Captain Malloy, and his one gigantic
tale of being ship's boy, his ear frostbitten
on a nineteenth-century whaleboat out of Niantic.

How he always rasped "That was the winter we walked
over the Sound, clear across to Montauk."

The ice is sweating now, like an upper lip.
A small lighthouse seems impossibly far.
Scraping and grating, floes begin to slip
perceptibly. A sudden snake-like scar

opens up, a grimace of chuckling waters,
black as oil. An envied gull sweeps grayly
into the sky. The shore is miniature,
horizon shifting beyond the breathing land.

Your story is cracking open without any thunder,
hatching the unformed darkness in which you see
your shadow bob and dissolve as light puts its hand
on your shoulder for the last time. And you slide under.

HEADING TO WILDWOOD

The dry heat wore a whippoorwill shoe,
on a crazy-veined map with Loveladies,
Barnegat. Soon, Ocean View
walloped the car with a real sea breeze
as Great Egg Harbor and Avalon loomed.
Egrets rose, lint above the marshes,
where prehistoric light stalked like doom
on bird legs through miles of razory rushes.
Motels of glass faced the coast of France,
where androgen waves were hurled and then withdrew,
licking the wordless stubble of the sand.
Light, ocean, and parents were all I knew.
Poetry then was still a kite in the skies,
tugging, tugging at all my earthbound ties.

Seashore Movie, 1960

We're pulling apart like the cartilage of an old film
that's torn and scratched, the burnt ocean flailing
with seams of white, high on amphetamines.
That was the beach, whose grains of sand are sparkling
in a strip mall parking lot miles inland.
Those were the gulls, manic in Hokusai blue
at noon, dipping and fluttering above the band
of rapid waves boiling as if someone threw
a switch for assembly lines in overdrive.
Those were the strangers, who wandered beyond the hill
in their glaring shirts of orange and red. Alive,
but now dispersed like atomic particles.
Those were the bodies, slim and beaded with water,
Chaplinesque in the vanished salty air:
mother and father, as young as I am old,
faultlessly holding up the tent of the world
while the child combs for slipper shells and stones.
Their quick, confident glances toward the unknown.

JERSEY SHORE

Scabbard, halberd, gem-encrusted swirls
on bituminous slopes, and breakwaters, skinny skeins
of darker ink, the not-to-be-walked-upon wing,
varnished by a lucent moon as the engine purls.
At each western window, sunset furls
its sluggish banner of blue and tangerine—
and below is the tide of longing, what's unseen
and reluctantly relinquished where ocean curls
toward dazzling neural displays of the coastal night.
Atlantic City pinwheels and bits of lode
are neon decorations for the gaudy scene,
and coming darkness is the only guest in sight,
welcomed by seed pearls lining the conduit roads,
by buoys and hatpin boats in crêpe de Chine.

DELIVERIES

To cracked decibels of chorusing sparrows,
those alar crowds dismantled in the skies,
above a camouflaged park that day borrows
from children's books, the weathership still flies,
all hue and turnstile, spinning the spokes of noon.
And below, with starlit fender, blocking a street,
is the huge mug of a stranded rig, maroon
and gray, its donut wheels lacquered black.
Decatur, Jerome, Gun Hill, Webster, Mosholu:
the asphalt riptide pulls, the names dissolve
in deliveries made, and bills of lading lost.
They watched from windows, scanning the avenue
for signs that never came, of who would thrive
and who would fail, and what the years would cost.

New England Summer

This light declares an extreme of pedigree
north of wonder and the voiceless choirs
of neutered churches with their scholarly spires.
The luminous, nesting shores agree:
brocade of thunder and sequined homily
send out their ships in burgeoning, anthracite pairs
to bring shadow to window ledge and stairs.
A sunflower wears its agonistic bee.
A meadow shines with bits of broken glass.
As sparrows bend the silvery stalks of weeds
and leap into pools of pure titanium,
with a placard in the tailor's place we pass,
the day offers its blinding, redemptive words:
"Expert Alterations for Ladies and Gentlemen."

At Hull

The land emits goldfinches, like a wrecked
oscilloscope whose citron pulses flee
toward the ocean's pure *cantabile,*
vacant *nihil obstat* of Atlantic.
Unshorn marshes hunker down and listen
for the slovenly ochre babbling of the tide:
another summer's here and curled up inside,
noons hawking their turquoise wares glisten.
Beaches sprawl beyond the tensile reach
of actuarial marksmen in the steep
and blinding dunes, as waves hypnotically teach
that shoreline means reprieve, a weekend bash
for lingering festive crowds who nightly gape
at the candled moon with its embryo of ash.

CAROUSEL

Enameled horses bare their shiny teeth
in happy catatonia, and plunge
counterclockwise; the wooden stage beneath
is a whirling disc; above are pipes that lunge
and rise, mimicking the sweaty school
of flesh. A wide-eyed breeze comes off the sea,
and colors swirl like taffy being pulled
as the Wurlitzer blares a singsong melody.
Look behind! A synchronized herd stampedes,
riderless in salty air, the painted steeds
of ancient children gone to seaside graves,
threatening our summery dark with new arrival
(Come back! Come back!) even as the ending bell
scatters their hope like salt on bituminous waves.

HARBOR AT OLD SAYBROOK

Where pageantries of peril flow quickly,
a nightmare sea is breaking panes from below
with stunted fists, but the lid of ice is heavy,
and its fine ebony crazings barely show,
except near the burly pier. A translucent crust
on blackened caramel pulls from the pilings,
leaving a moss of dampness where the water crests,
sloppy tar with cowlicks of wave, leaping,
lapping, in faint starlight. Every sound
skitters on stilts, or groans like a glacier calving.
In seaward darkness, a multiple birth of islands
rides the slick horizon; a ship's bell rings.
The body, like a pharaoh, covets the frost.
At two degrees, things are preserved, not lost.

AT MARCONI STATION

Perhaps to be distant is, after all,
only to grow smaller and invisible
as any star, to be inaudible
to others. The new gazebo's sky-rich wall
and absent windows announce that space is frail
and conquerable, open quadrants filled
with a furious tempest blue, chalk encircled.
He knew distances were animate and full,
words were migrant flocks. The air, decoded,
emptied its pockets of messages on land
where the dunes slope down to desperation,
and like a primitive typesetting, outmoded,
popsicle fences scatter on the sand,
fallen armies defeated by the limit of ocean.

In Franconia

A slag of broken mirror is semaphore
in mountain fold, like shock of glitter shale.
And shadow wreckage slips from peak to floor
as if the clouds are miming a sudden school
of coral fish in underwater coves—
the sea is gone, become a breathable blue,
but the seabed look remains—and current shoves
the stunted prickle pines, a retinue
that crowds the canyon ridges. Above those stark
and restive villages of boughs, a plane
like a tug tows a silhouette of shark,
then lets it go; it glides a silent lane,
surveying what the Andes will become:
weathered cuprite and stunned viridian.

CLIMB

Where contour lines are close, the way is steepest;
this one learns from topographic maps
with their circled hills and terraced flanks, darkest
where sienna lines adhere, like Mayan steps.
Our roughened slopes, in looking back,
were features of affection—and your words,
unrehearsed, just words of that giddy panic
setting in as the air thins upward.
In the forest, hatch marks of light make every tree
a negative of birch, as if some Cézanne
of the rootless stars had passed this way,
daubing distance with trail marks of perception,
as granitic paths beneath a tattered canopy
lead us on to overlooks and quandaries.

GOETHE AT NAPLES

The sky is overcast, and a sirocco is blowing,
as if the grasses were compelled to write
an invisible page, and then another—
a weather for writing letters.

I've seen too much: rabble and beauty,
astonishing horses, dazzling fish.
Everywhere, the heaving sides of life,
with touches of sweat, and oil and sea.
And paintings one needs a candle to find
in churches smaller than books.
Each picture is like a cracked maze,
or a blackened map. Ugly at first.
Then one notices a single hand, or an eye,
a glimpse of one's beloved in a crowd.

The memory of Rome is like an old
dilapidated monastery, badly placed
on piddling flats that smell of sewage
and senile empire. Here, the sea
lets the land breathe toward Palermo.

The lungs of a frigate fill—
like a saint's—all will, the body flayed
and gone. That's how the ancients seem to me—
skeptic, emboldened, fleshless.
Between Cape Minerva and Capri
the boat disappears—if I were to watch

a person I loved sail away like that,
I wouldn't survive it.

The harbor waves are frisky in the wind.
Like the noble horses, yesterday,
threading dirty streets—
my heart went out to them—
a line of straggling gold,
varicose vein of ore in dull hills.

This is a world where psalms make sense,
though the earth is changeable as weather.
Don't think of certain dangers,
especially one of which I needn't speak.

I enclose the envelope of your last letter,
scorched in one corner.

AT SAND KEY

The lighthouse, like a manikin of wire
or badminton shuttlecock, is stuck seven
miles out where mild onslaughts of water
are sluicing through its latticework, an open

sea-cage. Shaken, with its dormant bell
of light, by tide's pile-driving thunder,
there's nothing inside; nothing can be held
or turned away, so nothing is lost. The labor

and cost are rust and wounds within the reef,
legs of iron where fragile rooms might be,
epilogues of rain without any grief
above the wall-less caverns of the sea.

Imagine tailors basting a gown of waves
that slips, is pinned again in sliding air,
a voluminous satin drape that never behaves
in slapstick of the hurricane whose flair

for rearranging and estranging bullies
its way up from an always billowing south.
Or stars dissolving in transient gesso pools
that lap against the massive iron hooves.

Out where the booby with fishing-goggle stare
rests its rubbery feet on those barrel hoops

(a guess, for photographic proof is rare),
boats make blindly energetic loops

that fade like braided rope in a vat of dye.
Dwindling toward the Gulf is *Ecstasy*,
its wake a pattern fastened to the sea,
watched by a blinking, tearless Cyclops eye.

Old Keys Highway

A glance across induces vertigo.
That skinny *doppelgänger*, the old bridge,
within waving distance, but abandoned years ago,
sections suddenly missing, a crumbling ledge.

On precarious stilts, pretending to dignity,
it ribbons close to us, then stumps away
on its own demented voyage out to sea,
then stops. Maybe it costs too much to pry

from its coral boots. Maybe the birds like it,
and roost unseen at night on their private El.
But fear of -ectomies and fear of height
make it seem a souvenir from hell,

memento mori on shuddering crane's legs,
of ropeless severings—for fifty feet's
as far as Rome. It doesn't matter who begs
to cross the staring absence of a street:

here is limit, a plunge or a panicked save,
a concrete archipelago that insists
despair is how desire must behave,
a seminar in nowhere for idealists.

A piece that still attaches in the east
has a tiny gate blocking the runner's path

with X: a double *defense de* nothingness.
It has the roughened lip of aftermath,

where strata are exposed like layer cake.
"This is how our roads were made in A.D.
fill-in-the-blank." There must be some mistake.
The road I need to take is entropy.

Somehow I'm marooned out there in time,
coming to the jagged edge of all that is,
and back the way I came, finding the same,
stories above the bright and lethal sea.

Islanded on a span where no one's been
for decades, finding only a gull's bone
picked clean, an odd feather of ultramarine,
a doomed tree proving some law of dispersion.

Stars are gritty sand on burnished black,
a reef is a hidden bruise steeped in blue.
Now there's no way forward and no way back
when the tide whispers sudden news of you,

a thought fierce and ruptive as any storm,
alive in a fluorescing city on the rim of sleep.
The moon is a vacant clock, the diver a form,
and no one there to applaud the soundless leap.

FIRST VIEW OF SIBERIA

Shed some tears for the sin of altitude,
the obvious treachery of the maker of shapes—
his monstrous concern for patterns vast and crude,
never the fibrillating wing and crushed nape.

Tributaries shoot out where tubes of gesso
were punctured. Then, those dragon forms of white.
Rivers, maybe. And black de Kooning strokes
scattered around like fingerpaintings of night.

At last, the icebox door of a word opens—
and nothing fanged, booted, or bloody emerges.
The landscape below is thrillingly benign:
a few suturings in snow, no trace of purges

above the unmarked graves of poets, lovers
of wine and ice cream who died among the wolves.

The Road to Sheremetyevo 1

Our van, daylight's incubator, jolts
the darkening road where dusk is clearly gaining,
a seepage of ink from fairy tales. Bolts
of lightning are riddling the distance where it's raining.

Those navy clouds, like incense from a church,
dead-ringers for Rasputin's eyebrows or baby tornadoes,
drag across the stands of shimmering birch,
candled trees lit by a noon without shadows.

What is trivial becomes an eternal tableau—
a dog in a stand-off with a smaller animal,
or a blown paper in a field of churned-up soil.
Time loosens the image and lets it go.

For this, I've traveled halfway across the earth,
turning now, to see a mud-colored, mute
mail truck out of the dustbowl in pursuit,
with letters addressed to me before my birth.

READING CYRILLIC

Scaling the dark cliffs and broken columns
for a sudden view (the lens wildly swung)
of gleaming fragments of that whitest sea,
page between bars, requires pickaxe, geology.
Here a lintel's cool Doric shade,
there, a helmet's curve. On the steppes,
a pony turns toward an east of its own.
In a monastery, an empty window.
Someone rides, swirling a sword above his head,
stopped by the frozen north of type.
Lines are nomads in their ornate tents,
or inscriptions, chiseled and immense.
In the mind, ice floes starting to break up
announce the spring of meaning, like gunshot.

BRIEF HISTORY OF A CITY

First, the clattering down of birches, like staves.
Then the layout, like ice cubes seen under water.
By a sutured railroad track, a smattering of graves.
Dresses—by train from Paris—made to order.

Wars in which stairwells rage and buildings crumble.
Flocks of speckled birds caught in the trees,
rising up like dust as artillery rumbles.
Rain rivering the window after disease.

Placid days of nursery school and parks.
From a rusting balcony where no one declaims,
a page of homework swirling down, its mark
a deliberately penciled "Good!" near a child's name.

Along the prospect, enormous billboards sport
a giant chicken or bottle. The future survives:
cars pull away from squealing stops with a snort,
past traffic signs where stick figures flee for their lives.

On Seeing the Heroic Statue

Here, where space is fastened down for good,
and gray is an element added to water and fire,
air and earth, a soldier in a pointed hood
who's looking vaguely Byzantine admires

a martial vision seething in the west though not
the Spartan Greeks, whose marbled delicacy—
childlike to him and serene—he would call sissy,
for what's a naked foot to a massive boot?

The blown cape of stone refuses to give,
as if the wind itself weren't free,
and a rifle butt has found an adjective

to teach a lesson about how things will be.
His shadowed stare rules us out by decree.
There is nothing here that sees the way we live.

Spring in the Taiga

A screen of birch allowing the sky to appear,
recklessly, like a negligee worn in the arctic.
No more mile-high ice of a locked-up year
in the Pleistocene, but these slender branches click
like castanets when January tries its frozen
harmonica and no living thing
saves another except for sociable, treacherous man.
Where water sellers are stacking bottles and giving
change, women and children tread soft paths
into a doorless forest; the curtain of the north is pulled
aside for the stilled ballet of trees, for a swathe
of scribbled chalk where tiny redstarts trill.
Soon, off the scimitar beach that winter rescinds,
a sail like a tentative hand will be shaping the wind.

NATURAL THEOLOGY

Neglected ministries of the fertile bank
claim this as their hive of rest, not busyness.
Who holds the world to his ear and shakes it, thanks
the music of unsynchronized things, and rests
where the weeds pray with so many hands
the church of day is jammed.
Sun shoves its sack of glitter at the land.
Billowing, rushing thunderclouds, not lambs,
not faces, ravage Hopkins's wind-walks.
A golden tower is a Byzantine spy
who parts the branches of the trees and balks
at the relentless, hurrying fronds, asks "Why,
where is your design, inconsequent pain?"
In the border towns of thought, a fine rain.

Near the Waterfall

I riffle those leafy Amazonian files
for lives scribbled to stillness—like Leonardo
perhaps, his whirlpool drawings in embryo—
finding only forest in sunlit coils.
Where slithery torrent ducks slide the falls,
all I can see is green flanking the road,
and listen as a vertical sea shudders to explode
on hidden rocks, dousing antiphonal calls
of treetop birds. The air is milky with mist,
where molecules of the dead are newly loosed
in sky's amoral heaven for a rainbow's use.
Everyone is preserved, but there is no list
as the forest pens, with nothing like dismay,
sumptuous algorithms of decay.

DECEIT

The trees, like ravaged legions, point accusingly
at invading armies of the wind. After so many years
they still remember their first winter's brutality
and betrayal. No longer crowned with leaves at their ears,

in a triumphal saga of seed and sun, but with ice,
stripped of whatever burgeoned by the tyrannical cold,
bested, battered, left to their own devices—
a ravaging and drawing in—becoming old.

They remember when the handsome sky was a blue desk
where they rested their heads, like tousled Renaissance boys,
the page open to curlicues of botanic text
about what would come next, spring (that rot) and its joys.

The earth, ashamed of the seedbed's price, never said
what a lie she'd spun, and what would happen instead.

ZOO LESSON

In lassoed Africa set down like a dusty prize,
pacing his chiaroscuro crypt—from acid bath of sun
to that dank, basement jail—the switch of his tail a haywire
ink brush lazily wielded by a cobra—he'd stun

by shaking his huge skull and swiveling the glare
of topaz eyes whose slits would barely admit
the idea of your being before discarding it—
words clung to his hide like burrs: spoor,

feral, veldt, tawny, pride—the lope
and sway of his hips would suddenly fold and slump
to a silhouette not noble but merely bored.

Adults showed him off as if they had planned the world
and were offering its wonders to us: I felt sorry for him—
with his slack-jawed look that said *meat*—and wary of them.

GOETHE AT THE COLOSSEUM

On pagan parapets moonlight stalks
like a contrite priest saying his breviary,
carrying his private darkness like a sack
filled with ashes of the ordinary.

A sudden breeze is herding flocks of smoke
through all the woe-mouthed doorways, where huge crowds
stunned and shook the sky whenever they spoke
with a single blurred roar as dead men bowed.

Only something this massive can be seen
through time: legions pulling on their armor
as scattered domes of the bull-necked city gleam
and names of minor gods fade in the clamor.

Now flames of beggars flicker in these vaults.
Lacking another home, a hermit squats
in a chapel. Those whom history assaults
are living all around us—this is what

awaits any greatness that momentarily breaks
the greedy surface of our earth. Life
honeycombs the ancient stone and takes
whatever it needs. All is perpetual strife.

I'll memorize this place, for it's the model
of every failed enclosure and fallible heaven,

a dying monster exhaling through each nostril
on the second of February, 1787.

Who writes down what escapes and what remains?
Rome is gone. Again there were no games.

Opening Day

Two shots—the first, a kind of condensed applause,
as if a baker clapped with floury hands, summoning
someone. In a tapestry, we see something twitch and pause
where the olive-colored wood begins, and the birds sing

silently. The second has more intent,
of pewter and white—like the sky holding its breath—
heading severely toward the dappled pattern it's meant
to still, and define with the charcoal outline of death.

In the ringing between, swallowed thunder. And snow
swirling in waves on an eye of glass, as the legs
begin to tremble. The hunter slams down the gavel.

Then no sound. No wind. Nothing begs.
In a weaving whose corner was soaked by rain long ago,
that vermilion thread, starting to unravel—

VISITOR

Slung below Arcturus like a swung
and suddenly stilled plumb, a myope's blur,
an eraser smudge on midnight-dipped vellum,
is that gossamer laggard of the calendar

called *comet*. Slow thrill for animists
who derive, from sky's vast playground
a sudden airless hope for some melodious
docking of the real and the imagined,

odd as sudden hives or a comb jelly
with lucent parachute. When it arrives,
(is it there or not?) a breath of chalk,

a bobble in the numbers, it survives
only to grow and brighten silently
like any grand passion in the absence of talk.

THAW

Winter sloth. Wildly weaving shallows
in the near distance, light polished to the gleam
of silver and pressed, aghast, at all the windows
while yapping crows circle the house like a tomb.
Weather's hauled in—from southern England,
where palm trees . . . but no, the cracked bread
of the coast grows sodden in sudden warm rain,
snow's depressed cousin. December's dead.
Till a freeze mortifies the scene again,
as buoyant rafts of neat, inscrutable birds
undulate toward Europe, the sky grows plain,
less near, and the point of crisp words,
distinct colors, boundaries—that shout *stop*,
pours in with the cold surf kicking up.

ORB WEAVER

The argiope, with pincers dipped in jet
scuttles a silken map, and then descends,
like a rock climber on belay, or acrobat,
a jockey discreetly dressed in Degas bands

of autumn colors turned up a few degrees
to scarlet racing stripes. Wind shimmier,
sack of inky nerves, scuttler down trees,
bonnet belly, rapid shiny dabbler,

poring over cloth for imperfections:
"This web inspected by . . ."; is that a tag
or tattered flag of evening's last confection,
milkshake moth? She suddenly feels the tug

and ripples, fluid as a leggy bird
on a vacuous trampoline to the gory scene,
to dispense swift needles on the ward,
a brusque, anthracite nurse bearing morphine.

Then swaddles a hexapod mummy in silk where
it hangs, cradled on a stalled Ferris wheel,
and taps out lullabies in the feral air,
harpsichordist of whatever spiders feel

after such a perfect execution.

ENDANGERED

Dragonflies everywhere, adept biplanes
whirring and flicking above tea-colored water
and phosphorescent grass which calms to lawn
where the panther, like a favorite toy, is soldered

to a base of stone. Stunned to be made of bronze,
diminutive and baffled in alertness,
caught in the open under shadow fronds
of tiny-headed palms, it slinks from smallness

rippling the armored suit of monument
that nothing can escape. The panther lives,
but sketchily, as muscular argument,
a twitch of sawgrass somewhere in the sieve

called Everglades, circling its own absence,
miles out, lithe and black as a hearse.

WRECKAGE

Last spur of the Andes or indifferent beak,
Cape Horn tears at the swirling air
jutting into hell; it picnics, where
rearing up on ribboned maps, too weak,
splendid caravels splinter and vanish
with an anaesthetic roar, rolling over
into the sea's book to be sealed beneath
the furred, rippling steel of its ceaseless cover.
Massive kelp beds lash them, like the hair
of a coppery corpse with ravaged face of water.
As they are pulled down with it in hacked shards,
flooding coffins, as thundering spouts pour,
tins and barrels fling their helpless words
at the small, flirtatious coves of the shore.

Dead Seal

First, the way-open jaws—as if to bite
down on the agonizing air blowing through gaps
where solid flesh once repelled the world and flight
was second nature: a sprinter's cold laps

through ocean currents the color of cartridge ink—
like an ichthyosaurus, partially sprung from stone,
or a traveler slaughtered a month ago on the brink
of rescue, whose ragged, gaping cry—"Alone!"—

would have crossed the species barrier but was foiled
to aftermath, a snakehead large enough
only for nightmare. Then why do we recoil
and blame you for the horror? Your cylindrical, tough

body the size of a baby, imperfectly swaddled,
eyeless now, its voice emptied out from a sack,
naked earholes the indifferent Master drilled,
whose monstrous skill astounds and distracts.

Dark dovekies scissor over the surf,
skimming your never-again-to-be-sensed domain
from which you were strangely expelled to this hostile plain
and hounded by frenzied worshippers at the church

of dissolution, the yammering gulls that soon
you could not see as they avidly pecked out your eyes,

their footprints whirling in a grotesque dance for the moon
to silver and the highest tide to swirl inside.

The blind anguish of your snapping is preserved
in the curve of your spine and scrape of your final bower;
even a god without empathy would be unnerved
at this huge cry frozen from your final hour.

The beach is deserted now and the gulls are missing,
the light slicking whatever is left of your pelt.
I tell myself I'll never endure what you felt,
but the neutral sea keeps hissing, hissing. . . .

AUBADE

Where, in thickets of evergreen
does the one-legged sparrow roost,
with backward glance—that shadow puppet seen
teetering on the ledge each day, its ghost
leg beneath a feathery stump,
a diagram gone wrong—
battling the civil wind,
an error nature can't rescind?

Tiny funambulist in constant
motion to keep an imperiled balance—
as night begins pitching its lightfast tent,
and pinpoint stars announce an arctic sentence,
as rampant cars are boiling past,
temperature plummeting fast—
does winter never fail
to ripple its lethal, silvery scale?

Extinguishings of day are soft
and treeless: the ruffled breast of a hawk
in gutteral snowstrike, trailing jess aloft,
charred against an eggshell sky, a hawk
whose eye is floating like the sun
centered with obsidian
beyond the barred cloud,
bringing a neutral, feathery shroud.

The sparrow dreams of Xanadu
for sparrows, and singing muffled vowels

that racket near the warm warehouses of noon
before the panels of summer flame to jewel
and shadows write upon the gleam
a poem sliding east
as gulls are flickering past:
"I hope the dangerous dawn comes fast."

PANGAEA

They shift with the grim enormity
of restless sleepers whose plates of bone grate
at skinless junctures; fine granite flakes
are stillborn sparks from these huge flints that try
again to light the fissures of the earth. Sea
invades the African east, a quickening lake
of aquamarine clarity, clambering to mate
with the soon-to-be-seabed, tropic Zuider Zee.
A pumice spine is raised in the white steam
of Iceland, where palatial greenhouses grow
and fog to pseudo-frost; earth's hypocaust
punctures with volcanic flare: charred rock splits
to glow, while far to the south, Greek villages gleam,
threatened by the sullen lurch of sea below.

CURRENT EVENTS

Trailed by the useless lifeboat of a shadow,
skimming the suede of sea or furrowed land,
metal sheets molded to the air's great hand
keep nosing westward. Stars are a big show,
and newly violet clouds. Here below,
in the east, the nightly homeless have fanned
out in urinous parks; a speechless band,
three men and a child, trundles a cartload
of bottles. The sound is like wind chimes,
the cart, a wicked centrifuge; a cough
nags from a landscaped school. And limousines
are liquid in the streets. Savage times
have crept up, and still the jets rise, taking off
with aquamarine accelerations.

CRUCIFIXION DETAIL

Hammered the cross. Two skinny martyred trees,
stunned by a new purpose for xylem, phloem.
Sunlight, same as now. The same decrees.
Hoisted arthritic bole and riddled grain.
Helmets shine on a distant hill. Progress
being made. A donkey pulls a cart
along the rutted road. A soldiers' mess.
Spooning their strange soup. Without any art
or fear of germs. Familiar squint at noon,
the one in textbooks of ethology.
They lust for town. Here, their work is done.
Wine and meat, the usual revelry
for the hapless body: auricle, bone, hamstring.
On the rim of sight, their own deferred dismantling.

Goethe in Sicily

The mind applies layerings of distance,
varying tints of Olympian blue.
Where the bones of mountains are showing through,
we find the artifice of permanence.

I no longer see nature, but pictures:
topiary gardens of oleander,
espaliers of lemon trees that wander
along classic streets designed for epicures.

Here, fish swim as if drugged in darkened pools.
In nacreous shade, they swarm like armies,
or baffled crowds that unwittingly build cities.
Compliant nature shadows ambient rules.

Lines of Homer dazzle the whitened page,
so unlike those rough, casual markings
the sea tosses up, its combers thudding
on beaches straight out of the Bronze Age.

Notes penned in desperation cannot last.
As clouds evade the finicky draftsman,
particulars find obliteration.
As patterns upon the sand are newly cast,

the wet, glistening sheet draws them back,
pulls them under, so swiftly dismembered

in that violent muscle flowing seaward.
I watched the shore's unforgiving arc,

and thought of Odysseus, sheltered, alive
on that island where two thickets intertwined.
A savage beauty rains down upon the mind
images of olive and wild olive.

PASSER

passer mortuus est
        —CATULLUS

Puffs of ash, or feathery galls of winter
breathing on the branch, sparrows crouch
in a midget apple tree, their scraggly bower
barely a canopy, open to the reach
of wind. (Cold fingerings of scapulars
and nape.) That chorusing and chorusing
is childhood's obbligato. As ivory air
conducts, all the ghostly sparrows sing
who clustered on our windowsills to share
pale breadcrumbs the wind would sweep away
like chaff. Their lives were traffic swoop and veer;
their uniforms of brown would soon decay
along the curbs, but each is found in that tone,
like archaeopteryx pressed in a book of stone.

Intimations

That huge roster made plausible by forgetfulness
down by the caissons of the watercolored bridge,
where the river, silted with metal, was sliding west—
no one could memorize it. The films began to age,
melting in their own catastrophes of departure,
a wood-burning kit taken to panels of sun,
miniature forests, roads with asphalt scars.
I knew something was brewing among the pigeons
as they shivered along the stoops, like wind-up toys.
Where the jets rose on the Island was where the seasons
began to turn, and summer, garrulous and quarrelsome,
would have to be led away by the gendarmes of August,
their epaulettes glinting against the cry of dusk,
their suits dark as the trunks of storm-lashed trees.

GENERATIONS

Corinthian finches on a taut wire strung
between library columns, their martyrdom
of shattered nests forgotten with the spring,
their sweet gabbling, a fizzy sonogram.
Slaty pigeons on the ledge of PHILOSOPHY,
like sculpted fishing weights, or Henry Moores.
The ornate razzle of ornithology
is unkind to birds. The template of bird endures
though throngs are born and forgotten over time.
Who writes *Seventeen Years Before the Muse*
or catalogues an arc of unprinted rhyme?
We go from being praised to being used,
as our gifts are reinvented in that crowd
upon the steps, whose future briefly is allowed.

WHAT THEY SAID ABOUT KILLER BEES

This fruit of a dark and ferocious coupling—
is it revenge for their slavery in Brazil?
The moon-enamored north grows voluble
as yellow lights of early warning swing.
Above sleek-boated waters they travel,
lifting, falling, like a rug being beaten.
Only this much is certain: they always win.
Of milky southern mountains, they've had their fill;
acetylene around the bone, they swarm
at evening's throat. When the living mask lifts,
can we tell cow, dog, or man? The cloud drifts
toward reimagined Africa. Fury
is their alibi. The white sky grows warm.
When will that dot appear, and multiply?

DUPLICITY

November's aortic trees, like specimens
of vascular branching held up to clinical light,
are unique, we say, but who would know again-
ness if it came? "There's the silhouette

of an elm I knew in the fall of '73."
The contorted apple-dancer on the hill,
minus the fluorescent sign tacked to its finery,
no doubt has its double in a scroll

where its ruddy minions await a killing frost,
and the squat, lichenous rock speaks so slowly—
a syllable an eon—the meaning's lost.
Maybe earth is tired of novelty,

and so repeats—although we can't discern—
the upward shriek of birch and droop of fern.

Living off the Land

We battened on dreams of the anaesthetic sea.
A shell pried open was sleep shuddering
in its limbless cage, a silver haul shimmering
in our nets, an inverted forest's aviary
still gasping in the crown of its watery tree.
We jettisoned our ballast of conscience, gave in
and condemned the battered brown fin
that tipped in shallow waters of the lee,
then turned for absolution to milkweed pods
jangling greenly in an infant squall,
purslane calligraphing the shattered roads.
At night, fires darkened our shabby walls.
Beneath shadows of untouched wings big
as sails, we roasted the earthbound, suckling pig.

POETS

From two spots near the blinding skytop
where maple leaves are knit like Kekule's rings
against the drumhead white of three o'clock,
the chickadees' deliberate antiphon—

one seesaw of syllables, then another
a fourth down the scale, unadorned,
like notes a composer jots in placid weather
when the mind clears—arrives as watersong:

d–a, a–g, d–
a, a–g; as an oriole
threadles in the distance, making woodwindy
loops marry French horn ghostings to a drumroll

muffled in the pines, bird and answer
bird, flawlessly aligned, move closer.

FALL

Look. The village of apples is under siege.
The russet advance—like Birnum—across the hill,
means the end of their known world: apple spill
and plunge to alien grass. By now they've aged

beyond the picking. And apples run very, very
slowly, because their sole experience of motion
is having been jostled on a branch, albeit in every
kind of weather, so they have the vaguest notion

of what escape might entail, enough to pretend
they're not at the mercy of fate and chance. So when
the old umbilicus withers to a stem, they go,
paratroops lacking a map to the land below.

Near the pinched gathering of its dark, unseeing eye,
one is speckled like a plum. Another endures
a deep, tarry gash the spelunking flies
visit, while one is no longer an apple, but spoor

from a tree. Even here, the range of fates
is dizzying: some are stemmed like giant berries;
one wears a highlight out of Velasquez;
Three shelter beneath an oak leaf: mates.

The apple's only plan— turn to the sun—
is useless now, like the leaves that hang, tattered,

in a chilly wind. Like an orrery undone,
the spheres are facing everywhichway, scattered.

And the tree, their only hope, is self-absorbed,
its bronze prayer flags fibrillating, its pose
that of a bending sage. When it's newly orbed
in spring, they'll be long forgotten, zapped to zeroes.

FRONT

The merlin's wing is Vandal to the sky
and plunging razor to the migrant wave,
shearing down the eyeless slope of "Die!"
as rough-winged swallows torque above their grave
to plunge and rise, kites with strings of air.
Even a butterfly's ragged path of toil
is revealed as deliberate art, a buoyant dare.
But when cascades of surf lay stunned, and squall
and storm, those muscled roustabouts, bear
the wreckage off, the bullying sea is all.
Blank, blank is the eyes' hypnotic sweep.
Signs of life have vanished beyond recall.
No one thinks of the merlin furled somewhere,
dark as a grain of thistle in remorseless sleep.

EARLY SNOW

The coming across and coming across in waves,
where a pine leans like a ship beyond rescue in fog,
and the lawn's a sudden dune but without the staves
of fence and sea-sharp air. Keeping a log,

an iron cauldron with its scare of umber stalks
scribbles cryptic comments like a Latin seer
as a jet's sound erupts in fits and starts
and even now, the melt begins to appear:

distended liquid stars—in which is distilled
the essence of clear-eyed departure—drip from the gutters,
like the body pretending to be an eternal clock

though in secret places now, starting to utter
its long haywire descent, tick by tick,
as flesh-colored leaves surrender on the sill.

FLOOD

Melting snow, tunneled through by water—
which is really water tunneling through itself—
looks like the inside of a birdbone or a crumbling shelf,
as a turbulent river gurgles through the ancient quarter

of a city lately scorched by fires, then quenched
by a blizzard, whose small charred dwellings seemed
to melt. Drilling rains came after, and drenched
whatever remained where thousands lately teemed,

and now, silt swirling like iridescent dust
or curling smoke, the river is torrenting through,
a small da Vinci experiment in the nature of current:

between granular banks and flow there is so much trust—
no entreaties, only a perpetual letting go to
a place where things you thought were certain, weren't.

GOETHE AT GIRGENTI

Our view of the past, intermittent like lightning,
restores little to us, neither the unease
of temptation, nor the thunderbolts of a spring
grown cold among the headless deities.

On penciled Delphic crags, in oracular gardens
where a sarcophagus mutates to an altar,
where Hippolytus serves the unbelieving minions
of the dead, we find the mutinies of ardor.

How to choose between the Temple of Jupiter
with its disarticulated bones, and the blander
Temple of Hercules with its neatly sheared
limestone and flowerings of oleander?

As a wooden cabinet filled with Sicilian amber
clicks open, I see the colors of the shore—
opalescent honeys, hyacinthines, rubies,
the oddly blank and serene ivories.

A cloud billowing in the distance seems
the Carthaginian coast where fulminant wars
are only the work of brilliant figurines,
small, light-pierced battle scenes for scholars.

FIREFLIES

Jig-sawed in
among ragged branches of pine
are so many volts of cobalt sky
still bright at half-past nine when the fireflies
start winking on.

It's a Jules Verne
evening in a submarine
and we're clicking down to the depths of day
where life in a random and biological way
begins to burn.

Some are green
and cold as winter stars,
others like golden helicopters
are doubled, slow surges on the oscilloscope,
fading from the screen.

Bolides pulse
like a slowly widening eye
then close in carboniferous sleep
lanterning their way into dark decay deep
in the forest's side.

Here's one now,
a luminous warping spacecraft
or steadily growing satellite

sharply veering—a second before collision—
off into night.

Without a sound
fireflies fill the damp,
cool with endothermic desire,
gliding like amorous butlers on inscrutable rounds,
carrying lamps.

Or drifting up
like luminescent plankton
toward the stars that are nothing to them
because they seek the signal of themselves
and little else.

That we should stare
and find delight in their pattern
hardly matters; never knowing
they themselves are a language to be read,
a cryptic code,

the fireflies
are seeking love instead.
Deduce, from the presence of a heart,
though one so strange in all its lucid coldness,
a kind of art.

NOTES

"Bronze Age Helmet": Although Homer describes a boar's tusk helmet in the *Iliad*, and boar's tusks have been found in Mycenaean graves, I assume we do not know what Bronze Age helmets really looked like; my description is therefore a composite, with elements of Homeric helmets (bronze cheek pieces) and features, like incising, found in Greek helmets of later eras.

"Troy": Aulis and Thisbe of the Many Pigeons are two of the Greek cities from which the Achaeans derived their fleet, according to Homer's catalogue of ships in Book Two of the *Iliad*. Richard Lattimore's translation is "Thisbe of the dove-cotes" but Michael Wood uses the more demotic name in his book *In Search of the Trojan War*.

"Perseids": The Perseids is an annual meteor shower that peaks in the second week of August; it appears to originate from the constellation Perseus.

"Male": The star Aldebaren is the "ruby eye" in the constellation Taurus; the bull Orion seems to be hunting in the night sky; the horns of the bull can also be seen as the antlers of a stag.

"How the Crab *Iliad* Ends": Trulli houses are distinctive, whitewashed stone masonry dwellings with gray conical roofs that have white, decorative apices. Many are found in the village of Alberobello in the Puglia region of Italy. The De Soto was an automobile produced by Chrysler from 1928 to 1960 that was named after sixteenth-century Spanish conquistador Hernando de Soto. Thorazine is an anti-psychotic drug.

"Other": *Zinjanthropus boisei* (now *Australopithecus boisei*), an extinct primate discovered in Olduvai Gorge in 1959, was once thought to be an ancestor of humans.

"Anatomy Class": Andrew R. Syrbick (1936-2000) taught artistic anatomy at The School of the Museum of Fine Arts.

"The Cartographer": Richard Edes Harrison (1901-94) invented a revolutionary approach to mapmaking, called North Polar Azimuthal Equidistant Projection, which avoids the deceptive flatness of Mercator projection. In his system, the earth is arranged around a single point, the North Pole. As you move away from the Pole, equal distances from it remain equal on the map, but shapes and relative sizes of land masses and bodies of water become increasingly distorted. For many years Harrison's simple and elegant line drawings, done with a rapidograph, appeared in the *New Yorker*. His daughter died tragically in an earthquake in the early 1960s.

"Threescore and Six": Richard Curry Marius (1933-99) was a distinguished novelist and historian who taught at Harvard for many years; a scholar of the Reformation, he authored groundbreaking biographies of Thomas More and Martin Luther.

"Preparing for the Afterlife": Canopic jars were used in ancient Egyptian funerary rituals to preserve the internal organs of the dead.

"King Vulture": The king vulture (*Sarcoramphus papa*) is a brightly colored New World vulture, second in size only to the condor, with a habit of soaring very high on thermals.

"Birding in Yucatan": *Volatinia* is the generic name of the blue-black grassquit, a small, seed-eating bird of the Neotropics.

"*The Gallic Wars*": Hueys were American helicopters used in the Vietnam War.

"Deliveries": Decatur, Jerome, Gun Hill, Webster, and Mosholu are names of roads in the Bronx.

"At Hull": *Nihil obstat* is a Latin phrase meaning "nothing stands in the way"; it was used by Roman Catholic authorities to indicate that a work was acceptable to censors.

"At Marconi Station": In 1903, a message transmitted from a Cape Cod wireless station by inventor Guglielmo Marconi was directly received in Poldhu, Cornwall, making it the first wireless message sent from America to England. The station, at South Wellfleet, continued in use until 1917, and today an observation platform marks the site at Cape Cod National Seashore.

"At Sand Key": Sand Key is an important navigation point for ships on the way to Key West Harbor. The Sand Key lighthouse, an example of the screwpile design invented by the blind Irish engineer, Alexander Mitchell, had to be tall enough to be visible over great distances and sturdy enough to withstand hurricanes. Completed in 1853, the skeletal iron structure replaced a masonry one that had succumbed to the great hurricane of 1846. The lighthouse has withstood major hurricanes, proving the design's effectiveness.

"Old Keys Highway": The railroad connecting the mainland to the Florida Keys was destroyed in the hurricane of September 2, 1935, when a train sent to rescue veterans working on a planned roadway was swept off the tracks by a massive tidal surge near Islamorada. Some of the railroad bridges were then modified and incorporated into the Overseas Highway that was completed in 1938. From 1978 to 1983, the highway was modernized and separated from these old bridges, some of which still stand alongside it and are used as fishing piers.

"The Road to Sheremetyevo 1": Sheremetyevo 1 is the Moscow airport that serves domestic flights.

"Brief History of a City": The city is loosely based on Novosibirsk, the capital of Siberia. Founded in 1893 at a site where a bridge could be built across the Ob River to accommodate the Trans-Siberian railroad, it was originally called Novonikolayevsk and renamed in 1926. In 1998, The Novosibirsk Regional Museum had an exhibition devoted to the early history of the city, when the elite, well supplied with luxury goods by rail, seemed intent upon creating a miniature Paris in their drawing rooms.

"Spring in the Taiga": Taiga is the Russian name for the boreal forest of Siberia.

"Near the Waterfall": The setting is Tequendama Falls in the Andes outside Bogotá, Colombia. A torrent duck is a sleek, long-bodied duck *(Merganetta armata)* that swims and dives in cold Andean rivers and streams, often those with rapids and waterfalls.

"Visitor": Arcturus is the fourth brightest star in the sky, an orange giant in the constellation Boötes.

"Orb Weaver": The argiope is a brightly colored spider that makes large webs.

"Endangered": A bronze sculpture of the Florida panther *(Puma concolor coryi)* by Philadelphia artist Eric Berg stands at the entrance to the Everglades National Park Coe Visitor's Center; the statue and center are dedicated to Ernest F. Coe, who proposed the park in 1928.

"Pangaea": "Pangaea" is the name coined by geologist Alfred Wegener in 1915 to describe the single land mass that split apart, eventually forming today's continents; his theory of continental drift led to the contemporary theory of plate tectonics. The Zuider Zee was a shallow inlet of the North Sea that extended into the Netherlands; part of it has now been reclaimed for farming and houses.

"Passer": "Dead is the sparrow . . ." from the third line in the third poem of the *Carmina*.

"Poets": In 1865, the chemist Frederick Kekule had a dream that enabled him to determine benzene's structure: a ring of six carbon atoms joined by alternating single and double bonds.

"Front": A merlin *(Falco columbarius)* is a small falcon that can accelerate dramatically in flight.

"Goethe at Girgenti": In April of 1787, Goethe visited Girgenti, a town in Sicily near the coast that is the site of several ancient temples.